Wetland Animals

Muskrats

by Margaret Hall

Consulting Editor: Gail Saunders-Smith, Ph.D.
Consultant: Charlie Luthin, Executive Director
Wisconsin Wetlands Association, Madison, Wisconsin

Capstone
press
Mankato, Minnesota

Pebble Books are published by Capstone Press
151 Good Counsel Drive, P.O. Box 669, Mankato, Minnesota 56002
http://www.capstonepress.com

1 2 3 4 5 6 09 08 07 06 05 04

Library of Congress Cataloging-in-Publication Data
Hall, Margaret, 1947–
    Muskrats/by Margaret Hall.
    p. cm.—(Wetland animals)
    Summary: Photographs and simple text introduce the characteristics and
behavior of muskrats.
    Includes bibliographical references and index.
    ISBN 0-7368-2066-3 (hardcover)
    1. Muskrat—Juvenile literature. [1. Muskrat.] I. Title. II. Series.
QL737.R666 H26 2004
599.35′79—dc21   2003008559

Note to Parents and Teachers

The Wetland Animals series supports national science standards
related to life science. This book describes and illustrates muskrats.
The photographs support early readers in understanding the text.
The repetition of words and phrases helps early readers learn new
words. This book also introduces early readers to subject-specific
vocabulary words, which are defined in the Glossary section. Early
readers may need assistance to read some words and to use the
Table of Contents, Glossary, Read More, Internet Sites, and
Index/Word List sections of the book.

Table of Contents

Muskrats. 5

Wetlands. 11

What Muskrats Do 13

Dawn and Dusk 21

Glossary 22

Read More 23

Internet Sites. 23

Index/Word List. 24

Muskrats

Muskrats are rodents.
They have large
front teeth.

Muskrats have long tails and short brown fur.

Muskrats have sharp claws on their front feet.
They have webbed back feet.

places where muskrats live

10

Wetlands

Muskrats live in wetlands in North America. Wetlands are areas of land covered by water and plants.

What Muskrats Do

Muskrats swim and dive in the water.

Muskrats build their own homes. Some dig dens in riverbanks. Others make lodges out of sticks and mud.

Muskrats build rafts from reeds. They sit on the rafts to eat.

Muskrats eat cattails
and other water plants.
Muskrats also eat frogs,
fish, and clams.

Dawn and Dusk

Muskrats look for food
at dawn and dusk.
They sleep in dens
or lodges during the day.

Glossary

dawn—the time of day before sunrise when it is still a little dark

den—a place where an animal lives; a den can be a hole in the ground or a cave.

dusk—the time of day after sunset when it is almost dark

lodge—a rounded home made of sticks, rocks, and mud; a lodge has an underwater door.

raft—a floating platform; muskrats build rafts out of reeds.

rodent—a mammal with large, sharp front teeth; muskrats, beavers, mice, squirrels, and rats are rodents.

wetland—an area of land covered by water and plants; marshes, swamps, and bogs are wetlands.

Read More

Kalman, Bobbie. *What Is a Rodent?* The Science of Living Things. New York: Crabtree, 2000.

Loughran, Donna. *Living Near the Wetland.* Rookie Read-About Geography. New York: Children's Press, 2003.

Nichols, Catherine. *Wetlands.* We Can Read about Nature! New York: Benchmark Books, 2003.

Internet Sites

FactHound offers a safe, fun way to find Internet sites related to this book. All of the sites on FactHound have been researched by our staff.

Here's how:
1. Visit *www.facthound.com*
2. Type in this special code **0736820663** for age-appropriate sites. Or enter a search word related to this book for a more general search.
3. Click on the Fetch It button.

FactHound will fetch the best sites for you!

Index/Word List

build, 15, 17
claws, 9
dawn, 21
day, 21
dens, 15, 21
dig, 15
dive, 13
dusk, 21
eat, 17, 19

feet, 9
food, 21
fur, 7
live, 11
lodges, 15, 21
North America, 11
plants, 11, 19
rafts, 17

reeds, 17
riverbanks, 15
rodents, 5
sleep, 21
swim, 13
tails, 7
teeth, 5
webbed, 9
wetlands, 11

Word Count: 114
Early-Intervention Level: 13

Editorial Credits
Sarah L. Schuette, editor; Patrick Dentinger, series designer; Scott Thoms, photo researcher; Karen Risch, product planning editor

Photo Credits
Allen Blake Sheldon, 4
Brian Gosewisch, 12, 14
Bruce Coleman Inc./Scott Nielsen, 1
Corbis, 8; Paul A Souders, 18
Index Stock Imagery/B. Gillingham, 16
Tom Stack & Associates/Diana L. Stratton, cover; John Gerlach, 20
U. S. Fish and Wildlife Service, 6, 10